Bloodsucking Creatures

Bloodsucking Creatures

Anthony D. Fredericks

Watts LIBRARY™

Franklin Watts
A Division of Scholastic Inc.
New York • Toronto • London • Auckland • Sydney
Mexico City • New Delhi • Hong Kong
Danbury, Connecticut

For Marti Sherman—extraordinary colleague and special friend!

Note to readers: Definitions for words in **bold** can be found in the Glossary at the back of this book.

Photographs © 2002: Corbis Images/AFP: 6; Dembinsky Photo Assoc.: 38 (E.R. Degginger), 45 (Anthony Mercieca), 22 (Gary Meszaros); Dwight R. Kuhn Photography: 44; National Geographic Image Collection/Darlyne A. Murawski: 5 right, 27, 35; Peter Arnold Inc.: 18 bottom (Nicole Duplaix), cover (Hans Pfletschinger), 2, 11 (Gunter Ziesler); Photo Researchers, NY: 42 (Scott Camazine), 37 (Jean-Loup Charmet/SPL/SS), 14, 18 top (Stephen Dalton), 40 (Eric V. Grave), 16, 17 (Syd Greenberg), 12 (Rexford Lord), 30, 31 (NIBSC/SPL), 28 (James H. Robinson), 10 (Erich Schrempp), 29, 34 (Andrew Syred/SPL), 24 (Kenneth H. Thomas); Stone/Getty Images: 32 (Tim Flach), 9 (Yorgos Nikas); Superstock, Inc./Kunstmuseum, Bale, Germany: 19; Tom Stack & Associates/Tom & Therisa Stack: 5 left, 21; Visuals Unlimited/A.M. Siegelman: 39; Woodfin Camp & Associates/John Eastcott/Yva Momatiuk: 47.

The photograph on the cover shows a mosquito sucking blood from a human arm. The photograph opposite the title page shows a vampire bat in Argentina.

Library of Congress Cataloging-in-Publication Data

Fredericks, Anthony D.
    Bloodsucking creatures / Anthony D. Fredericks.
        p. cm. — (Watts library)
    Includes bibliographical references and index.
    ISBN 0-531-11967-X (lib. bdg.)   0-531-16598-1 (pbk.)
    1. Bloodsucking animals—Juvenile literature. [1. Bloodsucking animals.] I. Title. II. Series.

QL756.55 .F74 2001
591.5'3—dc21   2001017564

Contents

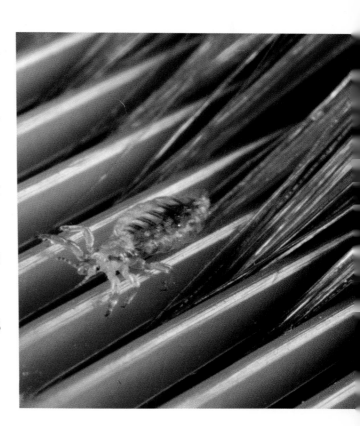

These bedbugs have consumed several times their body weight in blood.

Chapter One

What's for Dinner?

Have you ever had nightmares about things crawling on you at night? You may not want to think about it, but there are probably creatures living in your bed right now, and they creep and crawl over you almost every night. These creatures are known as bedbugs, and yes, they are bloodsuckers.

Bedbugs live in the cracks and crevices of bedding material. They are reddish-brown in color and are no larger than this capital *O*. Bedbugs do not live on us but near us. They are **nocturnal** animals that come out at night—when a warm human being is nearby—and rest during the daylight hours.

When a bedbug locates human skin, it inserts its mouthparts in three or four separate places until it finds a spot where the blood is close to the skin's surface. It feeds for 5 to 10 minutes—quite rapidly for a bloodsucker—and moves on. The bedbug leaves behind very small puncture wounds, each surrounded by a raised red spot.

A Ready Supply

There are thousands of different **species** of bloodsuckers in the world today. Blood is a readily available food source simply because there are so many animals with blood supplies. Bloodsuckers have specialized mouthparts that allow them to feed on much larger animals. These mouthparts can not only penetrate the skin of animals, but also suck up the rich blood flowing through veins and arteries.

Blood is a very nutritious food source. It contains valuable **proteins** that are important for cell growth. Bloodsuckers maintain proper body fluid levels by processing the liquids in blood. They also use **dissolved** solids in blood—such as **glucose** (a sugar), **amino acids**, and various **enzymes**—for nutritional purposes.

There is one problem that all bloodsuckers must overcome before they can consume liquid meals. If you have ever cut

The Red Stuff

About 55 percent of all blood is **plasma**, a pale, yellowish fluid in which three components are suspended. **Red blood cells** (the donut-shaped objects in this picture) carry oxygen around the body. **White blood cells** (the round object at upper right) help fight infections. **Blood platelets** (at upper left) aid in clotting. On average, an adult man's body contains 6 quarts (5.7 liters) of blood; an adult woman has about 3.5 quarts (3.3 L). The total circulating blood volume of a human is about 8 percent of his or her body weight. Thus, if you weighed 110 pounds (50 kilograms), your blood would weigh 8.8 pounds (4 kg).

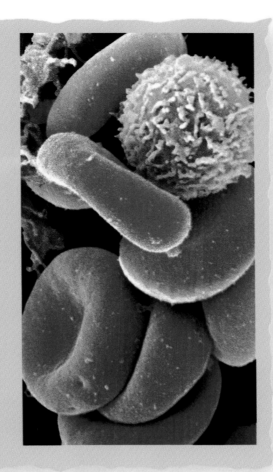

yourself, you know that blood begins to clot at the site of a wound. This is a normal and natural process in all animals with a **circulatory system**. Clotting protects the body from losing large amounts of blood.

Clotting would normally prevent any bloodsucking animal from getting the blood it needs. Most bloodsuckers introduce an **anticoagulant**—a chemical that prevents blood from

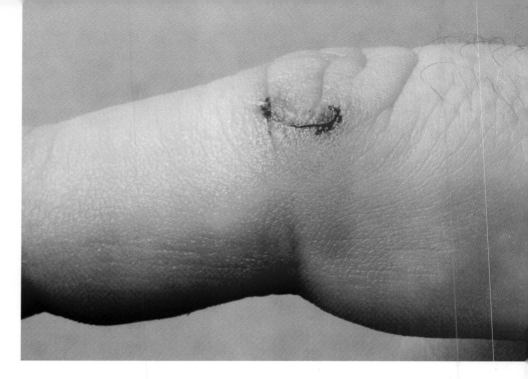

Soon after the skin is broken, blood begins to clot around a wound. To prevent blood from clotting, bloodsucking animals inject an anticoagulant into the skin before they begin to feed.

clotting—into their victims' system. Usually, this anticoagulant is mixed in with the bloodsucker's **saliva**. It allows the blood to flow freely from the wound or incision. As a result, the bloodsucker can drink continuously until it is full.

The World's Most Misunderstood Bloodsucker

The vampire bat is one of the scariest bloodsuckers. You might be surprised to learn that this animal is technically not a bloodsucker—it is actually a blood lapper. Vampire bats live in the tropical and subtropical regions of North and South America. These small animals grow to lengths of 2 to 3 inches (5 to 8 centimeters) and weigh about 1 to 2 ounces (30 to 60 grams). Vampire bats are among the world's smallest bat species.

Vampires

People in eighteenth-century Europe had many superstitions about creatures of the night. Some believed that all nocturnal animals were dangerous. Since these animals were rarely seen, descriptions of their habits and size were greatly exaggerated. Some of the best-known legends of this time concern a dreaded creature that attacked during the night. Assuming the form of a bat, this creature sucked the blood out of defenseless humans while they slept. Tales of this bloodsucker, known as a vampire, gave rise to the belief that all bats were bloodsucking animals.

Vampire bats live in colonies of up to two thousand individuals. Pictured here is a colony clustered in a cave in Argentina.

During the day, vampire bats hang upside-down in large caves or old mines. Their colonies include up to two thousand individuals. At night, they leave their roosts and search out victims. They usually attack domesticated animals such as horses, cows, mules, pigs, chickens, and goats. They also attack small wild animals. And yes, they have even been known to attack humans, but this occurs very rarely.

Vampire bats typically attack while their prey are asleep. The bat quietly sneaks up on a victim. Special heat sensors located just above its nose help it to select a spot, usually on the foot or the leg, where an animal's blood vessels lie close to the surface. It softens the skin by licking it, then makes a quick bite with its razor-edged **incisors** (front teeth). These specialized teeth make a shallow wound by slashing away a small

Two vampire bats feed on a cow's foot in Venezuela. The cow remains fast asleep.

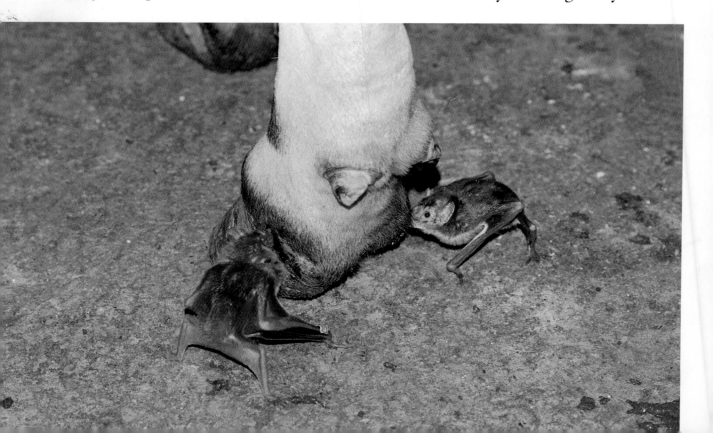

piece of skin. This incision is done so precisely that the victim does not feel it and never wakes up. Using its grooved, muscular tongue, the vampire bat laps up the blood that flows from the wound. Usually, a vampire bat drinks about 1 ounce (30 g) of blood from a different victim every night. Blood is the bat's entire diet. It eats absolutely no solid food!

As the bat feeds, special substances in its saliva prevent blood from clotting or coagulating. Scientists have discovered that the vampire bat's anticoagulant is twenty-five times more effective than any manufactured anticoagulant used in medicine. Sometimes a bat laps up so much blood that it is unable to take off and fly. Then it has to wait until some of the blood is digested before it can return to its cave to roost.

Monster movies suggest that vampire bats constantly attack humans, but in real life, that is untrue. In some tropical areas, vampire bats do occasionally bite people's hands or feet while they sleep. In areas where vampire bats are a problem, people sleep in beds surrounded by special netting that prevents bats from getting inside.

Three Different Species

There are three different species of vampire bats. They range from northern Mexico to central Chile and Argentina. The common vampire bat has twenty teeth. The white-winged vampire bat has twenty-two teeth. The hairy-legged vampire bat has twenty-six teeth.

A common cat flea burrows among the hairs on a cat's ear.

Chapter Two

From Small to Large

Bloodsucking creatures are found on almost every continent. They live in the deepest jungles, the highest mountains, and the driest deserts. Bloodsuckers also come in a wide variety of shapes and sizes. Some are as large as the fish you caught last summer. Others are as small as the dot over an *i*.

Bite and Scratch

Fleas are some of the most widespread animals on the planet. There are more than 250 species of fleas in North America alone. In the space of thirty days, one female flea can produce more than twenty-five thousand offspring.

If you have a dog or a cat at home, you are probably familiar with fleas. Fleas thrive in the ideal conditions on mammals' bodies. Mammalian hairs provide a good place for fleas to hide, and there is plenty of blood available for sucking. Adult fleas are small, flat insects, so it is easy for them to crawl among the hairs of an animal such as a dog. When a flea gets hungry, it stops and sinks its sharp **proboscis** into the animal's skin.

A flea's bloodsucking apparatus consists of a pair of pumping tubes attached to its mouth. One of these tubes penetrates the victim's skin and sucks up the blood. The other tube injects an anticoagulant under the skin to prevent the blood from clotting. This chemical makes the victim's wound itch when the flea is done feeding.

Fleas, like many other types of insects, go through four stages of growth: **egg**, **larva**, **pupa**, and **adult**. Some fleas grow from egg to adult in as little as one or two weeks. Other species might take as long as two years.

When a flea hatches from its egg, it is called a larva. This is a form that looks like a tiny worm. Each larva is about 0.25 inch (6 millimeters) long

Opposite: *The life cycle of a flea consists of four stages: egg, larva, pupa, and adult. Pictured here are flea eggs and some newly hatched larvae.*

Athletes and Acrobats

Fleas are amazing athletes. The average flea can jump 7 inches (18 cm) into the air and as far as 13 inches (33 cm) in a forward direction. In comparison, you would have to jump about 250 feet (75 meters) high and 450 feet (135 m) forward to equal the feats of the tiny flea. Pictured here are a flea leaping (right) and a flea starring in a tiny circus (below).

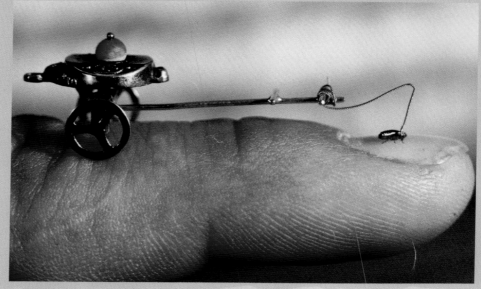

and lives almost exclusively on a diet of dead skin, hair, and digested blood from the adult flea's **feces**. After a short time, the larva spins a **cocoon**. Now the flea is known as a pupa. The pupa stays in its cocoon for a week or so.

If the pupa detects **carbon dioxide**, a gas that all mammals exhale, it is stimulated to hatch. It then emerges from its cocoon as a hungry adult. An adult flea must get a supply of blood within a few hours or it will die.

Fleas are dangerous because they spread diseases rapidly. When a flea sucks the blood of a diseased animal, it also sucks up the bacteria that live inside the creature's body. The germs multiply quickly inside the flea's intestines. When the flea bites another animal, some of the germs are transferred into that animal's blood. Now that animal is infected. More fleas bite that animal, and then each of these fleas bites other animals. As a result, many different types of diseases can spread rapidly through animal and human populations.

During the Middle Ages, more than 25 percent of the people in Europe died in an epidemic known as the Plague or the Black Death. Fleas that lived in the fur of infected rats spread this deadly disease. Large populations of rats were common in the houses and cities of the time, and

The Plague, a disease spread by fleas that lived on rats, killed more than a quarter of the population of Europe in the Middle Ages. Here, the horror of the Plague is portrayed in La Peste *by Swiss painter Arnold Bocklin.*

people did not bathe as often as we do today. As a result, living conditions were dirty and unsanitary. This created a perfect breeding ground for rats and fleas.

Traveling Bloodsuckers

When you travel, you probably use a car, bicycle, skateboard, or airplane. On your way to your destination, you probably do not destroy your vehicle. There is an animal that does just that—one that catches a ride with another animal and slowly kills its **host** as they travel together. This hitchhiker, the lamprey, is quite an unfriendly bloodsucker.

There are about thirty species of lampreys in the temperate regions of the northern and southern hemispheres. All lampreys begin their lives in freshwater. As they grow, however, some species move down rivers and into the ocean. The sea lamprey, one of the most common species, can be found throughout the Atlantic Ocean.

Lampreys resemble eels. They have slimy, scaleless bodies between 6 and 40 inches (15 and 100 cm) long. Instead of bones, their bodies contain **cartilage**, the same rubbery material that shapes human noses and ears. Lampreys have no jaws—their heads end in a large, funnel-like mouth. It is this mouth that makes the lamprey a fearsome bloodsucker.

The lamprey's circular mouth is filled with dozens of horny teeth. There are even teeth scattered across its muscular tongue. To feed, the lamprey searches for fish in lakes or

Old-timers

The ancestors of lampreys have been traced back more than 400 million years.

A Very Strong Mouth

The sucker mouth of a lamprey is so strong that it can pull itself up and over rocks or vertical walls.

rivers. When it locates a victim, it attaches itself to the side of the fish with its mouth, which is like a suction cup. Then it begins to scrape the fish's skin with its tongue and teeth. The fish begins to bleed, and the hitchhiking lamprey sucks up the blood.

Three lampreys get some blood to go as they ride on the back of a carp.

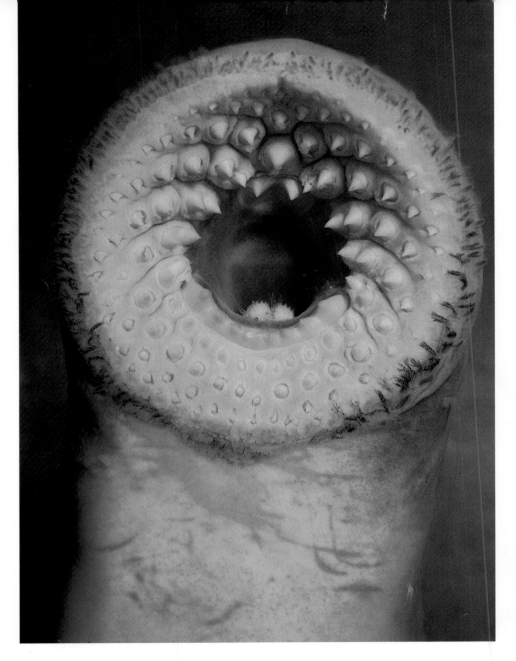

The circular, tooth-lined mouth of a sea lamprey is well adapted to the task of sucking blood.

Eventually, the lamprey obtains all the food it needs and detaches itself from its host. Sometimes lampreys continue traveling and feeding for weeks or months, or until the host dies. Lampreys spend much of their lives swimming as an attachment to one fish or another. Although they are capable of swimming on their own, they are more likely to hitch a ride on an unsuspecting host. This often turns out to be a death trip for the helpful fish.

In some parts of the world, such as the Great Lakes region of the United States, lampreys have become a serious ecological problem. They multiply very rapidly, attach themselves to large numbers of fish, and kill off entire populations of aquatic life. In recent years, a special poison has been developed to control this traveling pest.

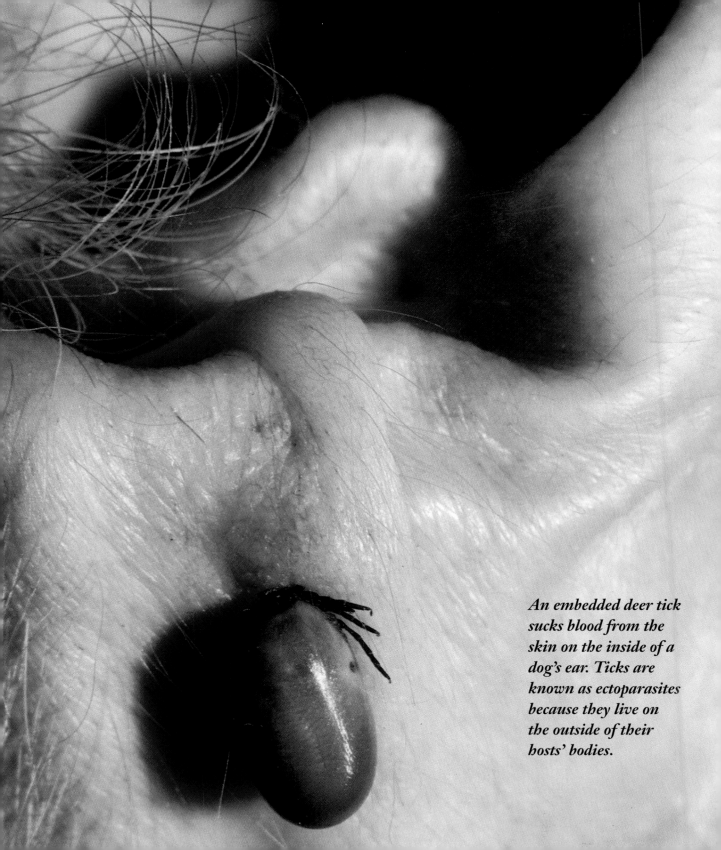

An embedded deer tick sucks blood from the skin on the inside of a dog's ear. Ticks are known as ectoparasites because they live on the outside of their hosts' bodies.

Chapter Three

Unwelcome Guests

Many bloodsucking creatures are **parasites**. A parasite is an animal that gets some or all of its nourishment from a host—another animal that provides it with food, shelter, or both. In most cases, a parasite harms its host in some way. Some parasites live with a host for short periods of time and then move on. Others stay with their hosts for extended lengths of time—sometimes their entire lives.

Scientists put parasites into two broad groups. **Ectoparasites** are organisms that live on the outside (the skin, hair, or fur) of other animals. Many of these creatures are too small to be seen with the unaided eye. Others are large enough to be picked off skin or fur. Fleas, ticks, lice, and lampreys are common examples of ectoparasites.

Endoparasites are animals that live inside other animals. They are frequently found in their host's digestive system, where they live and reproduce. These creatures are looking for a warm, comfortable place to live. Some endoparasites spread disease or drain their hosts of vital fluids.

A Full Meal

Scientists estimate that there are eight hundred species of ticks throughout the world. Most ticks fall into two basic groups: soft ticks and hard ticks. The difference is determined by the hardness of their outer bodies, or **exoskeletons**.

Ticks have eight legs and a flat body. They are not insects like fleas and mosquitoes, but rather are more closely related to mites and spiders. Like many of their **arthropod** relatives, ticks go through four stages of growth: egg, larva, **nymph**, and adult. In order to change from one stage to the next, a tick needs to eat a meal of blood.

Ticks cannot fly; they can only crawl. After hatching, a tick crawls up a twig or a blade of grass and waits. It can survive without food for a very long time—months, years, or even decades. This is known as **questing behavior**.

Ticks have a very poor sense of sight. They can, however,

detect other animals in their presence. They are extremely sensitive to carbon dioxide, which all mammals exhale. When a dormant tick gets a whiff of carbon dioxide in the air, it instantly becomes activated, even though it might not have moved for years. The tick then leaps onto whatever animal is passing by. A passing mammal might attract dozens of blood-sucking hitchhikers in a few minutes.

As soon as a tick lands on a victim, it scuttles beneath the fur or hair and buries the front part of its head, called a **hypostome**, into the skin. The host does not feel a thing as the tick injects an anesthetic and an anticoagulant under its skin. The tick continues to feed on the victim's blood for several days or

Ready to leap onto a passing animal, a dog tick has its front legs extended in the questing position. Ticks can remain dormant in this position, without food, for years.

27

Pictured here are two eastern wood ticks. The insect on the left is fully engorged with blood. The tick at right has not yet begun to feed.

weeks. As it feeds, the tick's body swells up to many times its normal size. Eventually it is so full of blood that it cannot drink any more. At that point, it loosens its head from the victim and falls to the ground.

Ticks are dangerous not because they are bloodsuckers, but rather because they are notorious **vectors**. A vector is an organism that carries diseases from one animal to another. Ticks do this by drinking blood from an infected animal and then drinking the blood of a healthy one. The infected animal's bacteria and viruses thrive in the tick's gut and are passed along to the next animal.

The Face Place

Mites are tiny insects found throughout the world. There are several varieties of mites, but some of the most distinctive are **follicle** mites, or face mites. Follicle mites can be found on almost every type of mammal in the world, including humans. In fact, you probably have several dozen of these creatures living on your face right now.

Follicle mites are long and thin. This allows them to live in very cramped areas, such as the follicle of a hair shaft. Human eyebrow follicles are particularly suited to these tiny creatures.

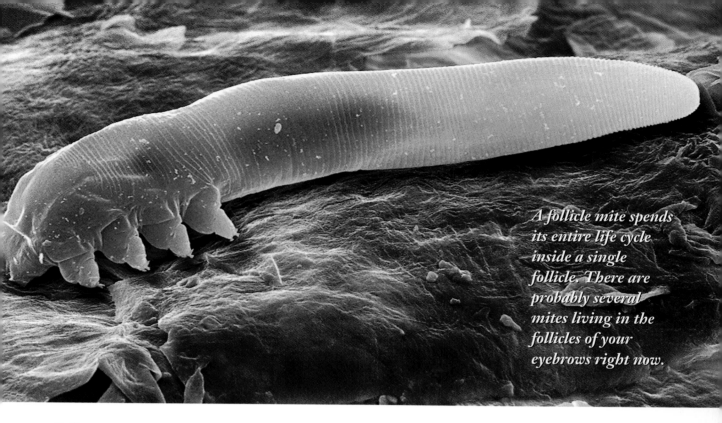

Like many insects, mites go through a process known as **metamorphosis**, during which they change from an egg into an adult. Young mites live in the same hair shafts as their parents. Entire generations of follicle mites can live, eat, breed, and die within a single hair shaft. Their life cycle is short—only about two weeks.

Technically speaking, follicle mites are not bloodsuckers. Instead, they dig into the skin of an animal and inject a special chemical. This chemical dissolves the animal's tissues, which form into a mushy mixture. The follicle mites suck up this mixture for a tasty meal. In a way, you could say that they are tissue suckers. Follicle mites have to eat almost constantly. Otherwise they will die.

Teeny, Tiny

Follicle mites are very small. About four of them would fit inside the period at the end of this sentence.

Fatal Flukes

This innocent-looking creature infects millions of people around the world. Known as the human blood **fluke**, it is one of a group of parasitic flatworms that includes more than six thousand species. This tiny animal ranges in size from about 0.2 to 4 inches (5 to 100 mm) long.

Flukes are simple creatures with only a mouth and a simple digestive system. They have no circulatory system and only a very rudimentary nervous system. They attach themselves to either the inside or the outside of a host with muscular suckers, hooks, or spines. Most flukes are **hermaphroditic**, which means that each individual fluke has both male and female reproductive organs.

Shown here are an adult male and female intestinal blood fluke magnified several times. The female occupies a groove on the male's back. Their heads are at upper left. These tiny bloodsucking creatures can cause liver and kidney damage in humans.

Blood flukes can be found living in a wide variety of **vertebrates**, including fish, frogs, turtles, and humans. Some flukes are ectoparasites, and some are endoparasites. A few are both—they can attach themselves either to the lining of the mouth or to the digestive tract.

Three types of blood flukes infest human beings—the urinary, the intestinal, and the Oriental. The urinary blood fluke lives in the veins of the bladder. The eggs of this creature bore through the veins and into the bladder, where they pass out of the body during urination. After a complex life cycle, they find their way back into the human body. For example, if someone handles contaminated materials and then eats without washing his or her hands, the flukes enter a new human host. There, they continue to multiply in the circulatory system.

The intestinal blood fluke is found throughout Africa and South America. The Oriental blood fluke occurs primarily in China, the Philippines, and Japan. These flukes live in the veins around the large or small intestines. Their eggs, which are carried in the bloodstream to various organs, often cause a number of internal difficulties, including enlargement of the liver. An infestation of flukes can be fatal if the worms occur in extremely high numbers.

This is a close-up of a blood fluke's head.

Head lice are only part of the zoo of microscopic creatures that infest the human body. Pictured here is a human head louse magnified twenty times.

Chapter Four

Humans As Hosts

Here is an amazing fact: Your body is a zoo! Right now, even as you are reading this book, there is an army of microscopic animals creeping and crawling on, over, and in your body. Some of them are permanent residents, while others just come around for an occasional visit. Even though you wash your hair and bathe, these animals are with you more often than you might like to think.

Lice Aren't Nice

Of the two hundred species of lice throughout the world, only three species attack humans. Perhaps the best known and most widespread type of louse (the singular form of lice) is the head louse. Head lice, which are related to body lice, need blood in order to stay alive. The human head is a perfect place for these creatures because it is warm and has plenty of places to hide. Best of all, the head has lots of **capillaries** close to the skin—an ideal situation for any bloodsucking creature.

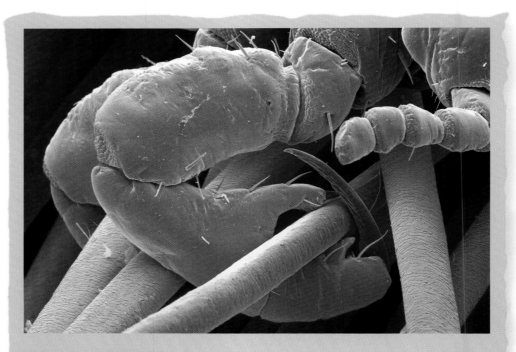

Strong and Fast

Head lice are equipped with very strong claws that allow them to grasp hair shafts and to stay anchored in one place. When they move, they can crawl quite rapidly through the hair. They cannot jump, hop, or fly as other types of insects can.

The life span of a louse is about thirty days. A female louse lays about 100 to 150 microscopic eggs, each about the size of a crystal of salt. The eggs, called **nits**, are cemented to shafts of hair by a special glue produced in the female's body. The female travels from hair to hair, cementing a single nit on each hair shaft. The nits will not hatch if they are placed on something besides hair.

After seven to ten days, the eggs are ready to hatch. Tiny babies called nymphs emerge from the eggs. Immediately after birth, the nymphs are hungry. They crawl down the hair shafts to the head and bite the scalp. After their first meal, the nymphs change color from transparent to reddish-brown—the color of the blood they have consumed. Over the course of the first nine to twelve days of their life, they change into adults. Adult lice need to feed on blood once every 3 to 6 hours.

A head louse crawls away from human hair toward a comb designed to get rid of the pesky insects.

People get head lice by coming into contact with other infected people. That means that a comb, brush, scarf, or hat worn by a person with lice can pass the creatures on to another person. Head lice must be removed with special combs and shampoos designed to kill both the lice and their nits. These bloodsuckers can spread to a whole group of people—a class of students, for example—in a matter of a few weeks.

Lovable Leeches

Long ago, doctors believed that people could be cured of many ailments and illnesses if some of their blood were removed. These physicians did not know as much about the human body as we do now. It was thought that if "bad blood" could be drained from a person, that individual would heal a lot faster. In order to remove the "bad blood," doctors placed bloodsucking leeches on the person's body and let them feed until they were big and fat. It was not unusual to use fifty or more leeches on a sick person's body.

Doctors still use leeches for medicinal purposes, but not for

Fascinating Research

Scientists are studying hirudin, the anticoagulant in a leech's saliva, as a potential blood-thinning medicine. People who suffer from heart ailments often take medicine to prevent their blood from clotting. These medications encourage the flow of blood through the heart and reduce the chance of heart attacks. Some researchers believe that hirudin might be more effective than some drugs currently being used.

the same reasons they did hundreds of years ago. Modern-day doctors use leeches to help people whose ears, fingers, or other body parts have been accidentally cut off and need to be surgically reattached. Doctors place leeches on the injured area. As they feed, the leeches keep blood flowing to the wound with an anticoagulant called **hirudin**. Hirudin prevents blood from clotting and keeps it flowing. As a result, the injured area receives a constant supply of blood.

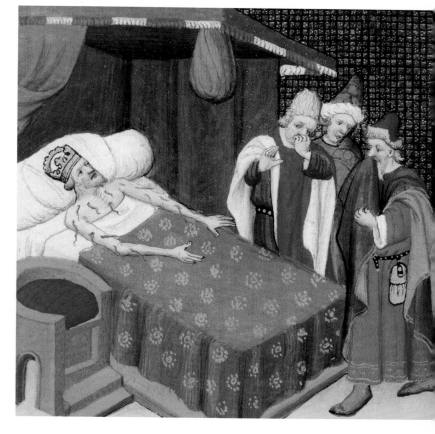

Leeches come in a variety of sizes, ranging in length from 0.5 inch (13 mm) to nearly 12 inches (30 cm). The largest leech, a tropical variety, grows to a length of nearly 18 inches (45 cm), about twice as long as a human foot. A leech's body has one sucker at the bottom and another at the head. These suckers attach the leech's body to its victim while it is feeding.

When a leech is attached to an arm or leg, it begins slicing through the skin with its three sharp jaws. As it cuts into the skin, it releases an anesthetic as well as hirudin. Now the leech can begin its feeding process. It either stays permanently

This illustration appears in a manuscript of Boccaccio's Decameron, *written in the 1300s. It shows the medieval practice of using bloodsucking leeches to treat disease. The patient in the illustration is the Roman emperor Galerius.*

A pond leech clings to the wall of a tank with its front and rear suckers.

attached or drops off after it is full of blood. A typical leech consumes about five times its body weight at one feeding.

Dinner on the Inside

One of the smallest yet most harmful bloodsuckers is the hookworm. Hookworms are intestinal parasites found in southern Europe, northern Africa, northern Asia, and parts of South America. People in tropical or subtropical environments become infected with hookworms through direct contact, usually by walking barefoot on contaminated soil.

Hookworm larvae live in the soil and penetrate the skin, frequently through bare feet. After they enter the skin, they

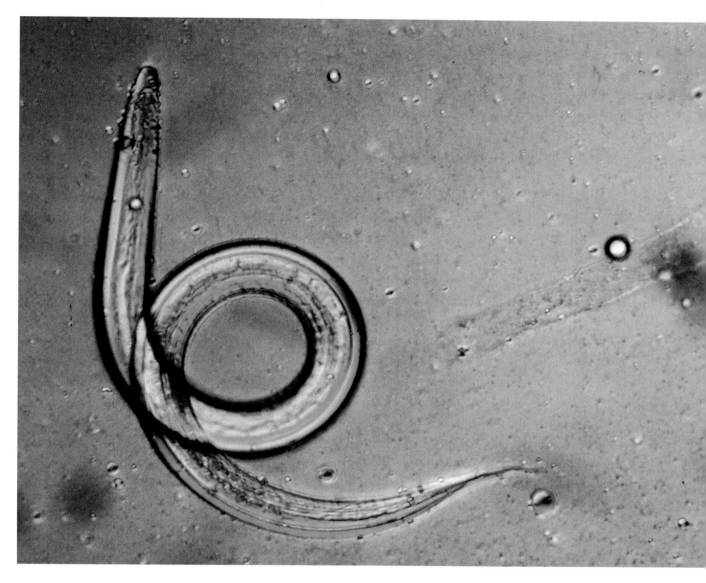

are carried to the lungs through capillaries. They live in the lungs for a short period of time and then migrate up the **trachea**, where they are eventually swallowed. Then they pass through the stomach and into the small intestine. This journey takes about one week.

The larva of a hookworm, magnified seventy times

39

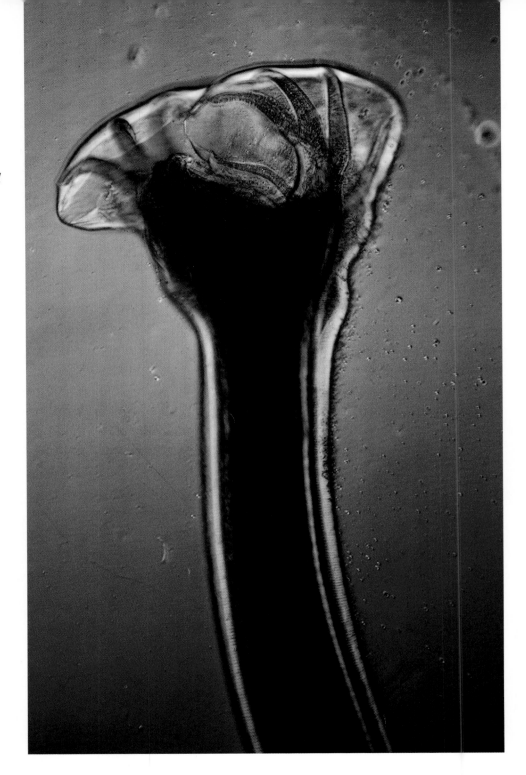

A hookworm uses its toothlike denticles to scrape away the protective lining of an intestine. This hookworm is magnified nineteen times.

In the small intestine, the hookworm larvae develop into worms approximately 0.5 inch (1 cm) in length. The worms have sharp, powerful toothlike structures known as **denticles**, which they use to scrape away the protective lining of the intestine. When the lining is punctured, the hookworm begins to suck the blood that travels through the intestine's tiny capillaries.

Using their denticles, hookworms remain firmly attached to the intestinal walls as they grow into adults. Adult worms produce thousands of eggs that are passed out of the host's body in the feces. If the conditions are right, the eggs contaminate the soil and develop into a new generation of infectious larvae in about five to ten days.

Millions and Millions of People

An estimated 1.3 billion people worldwide are infected by hookworms. This number equals approximately one-fifth of the total world population.

Blood Meal

People who are heavily infested with hookworms lose as much as 6.8 ounces (200 milliliters) of blood every day.

The deadliest-to-humans award goes to a common summertime bloodsucker—the mosquito.

Chapter Five

The Most Dangerous Bloodsucker!

The most dangerous bloodsucker for humans is a creature you have probably encountered during the summer months. This animal is responsible for far more human deaths than any other. According to the World Health Organization, more than 500 million people are infected with life-threatening illnesses spread by this

Song of Love

Have you ever heard the whining of a mosquito? The rapid beating of a mosquito's wings creates this sound, which is an important part of the life of mosquitoes. The antennae of male mosquitoes are very sensitive to the beating wings of females of the same species. Because females tend to be much larger than males, the wings of males and females beat at different frequencies. Males' antennae are equipped with special plumes that detect differences in sound intensity. Thus, males are able to distinguish the gender of other mosquitoes from great distances. They can also determine which females are members of their own species through differences in the sound frequency of their beating wings.

creature each year. More than three million people die every year as a result of being attacked by this tiny insect.

The deadliest bloodsucker of all is the mosquito, a word that means "little fly" in Spanish. There are approximately fifteen hundred species of mosquitoes. Not all species are bloodsuckers. Of those that do feed on blood, only the female does so. Female mosquitoes need the protein found in blood to produce their eggs, while males spend the majority of their life cycle sucking on fruit juices.

Worldwide Bloodsuckers

Mosquitoes are found throughout the world, from the Arctic to desert areas. Most species prefer the warm, damp conditions found in temperate or tropical regions. This is because most species of mosquitoes need a source of water—a puddle, river, stream, or lake—on which to lay their eggs. After two to three days, mosquito eggs hatch into larvae called wigglers.

Mosquito larvae, commonly called wigglers, hang from the surface of water.

These tiny insects feed on microscopic plants and animals in the water. It is only when they change into adults that they search out other food sources, such as blood. The typical mosquito's life cycle is three weeks to a few months.

In some parts of the world, mosquitoes are dangerous not just because of the diseases they carry, but simply because there are so many of them. In tropical countries with high levels of rainfall—and, thus, lots of standing water in which mosquitoes breed—mosquitoes multiply in great numbers. In tropical regions it takes only seven days for a mosquito to complete its life cycle from egg to adult. This means a new generation of mosquitoes matures every week.

When female mosquitoes are ready to lay their eggs, they swarm over the countryside looking for ready supplies of life-giving blood. Herds of cattle maintained by villagers are easy targets. In the Philippines, for example, a single water buffalo may lose as much as a whole quart of blood in one night—all as a result of constant attacks by swarms of bloodsucking mosquitoes.

Honing in on Blood

Bloodsucking mosquitoes locate potential victims through an elaborate set of sensory receptors at the end of tiny feelers called **palpi**. These organs pick up traces of carbon dioxide, as well as **lactic acid**, which is constantly excreted through sweat glands in the skin of many animals, including humans. Mosquitoes use these scents to determine whether an animal

A husky is plagued by a swarm of mosquitoes in Canada.

has blood or not. Their sensors are so accurate that mosquitoes can detect an animal's breath or sweat from a distance of 50 feet (15 m) or more.

When a mosquito locates a blood source, such as a human being or other animal, it lands on the skin and pokes its proboscis into a blood vessel near the skin's surface. The proboscis is similar to a very sharp needle. It is formed by interlocking mouthparts that quickly and painlessly penetrate the outer skin. Once it locates blood, the mosquito injects its saliva into the wound to prevent the blood from clotting. The itch that people get when a mosquito "bites" is an allergic reaction to the insect's saliva. Those itchy red bumps are

Drink Up

If you were a bloodsucker, how much blood would you have to drink to equal the amount that a mosquito can suck? Since a mosquito can consume two times its own weight in blood, you would need to be able to suck up two times your weight in blood to match the mosquito.

Here is how you can calculate it. For example, if you weigh 75 pounds, two times your weight equals 150 pounds. One pint of blood weighs 15.8 ounces (almost 1 pound). That means you would have to drink 19 gallons of blood to match a mosquito. The math goes as follows:

1 pint of blood = 15.8 ounces
Your weight = 75 pounds (1,200 ounces)
Twice your weight = 150 pounds (2,400 ounces)
2,400 divided by 15.8 = 151.9 pints
151.9 pints = 19 gallons (151.9 divided by 8)

places where mosquitoes have found a ready source of nutrition for their developing eggs.

Like ticks, mosquitoes are vectors. Many of the germs they carry cause serious diseases or even death. Mosquitoes are dangerous not because of their "bites," but rather because of the diseases they transmit through their saliva. Some of the most serious and life-threatening diseases in the world—malaria, yellow fever, and dengue—are transmitted by certain species of mosquitoes.

Preventing the spread of the diseases means eliminating mosquitoes. Scientists have developed special chemicals to spray on standing water surfaces such as ponds and puddles. These chemicals are designed to kill mosquitoes early in their life cycle, before they develop into adults.

Control of mosquito populations also occurs naturally. Mosquito larvae are part of the diet of fish, beetles, and newts. Birds, dragonflies, and hornets prey on adult mosquitoes. Mosquitoes are also a major part of the diet of a creature you met early in this book—bats. Since mosquitoes are nocturnal creatures, they are a ready food supply for many species of bats. In fact, if it were not for bats, our skies might be blackened by a constant swarm of mosquitoes. Look at it this way: the most misunderstood bloodsucker is protecting us from the most dangerous bloodsucker.

Glossary

adult—the fourth and final stage in an insect's life

amino acids—the substances that make up proteins

anticoagulant—a substance that prevents blood from clotting

arthropods—a group of animals with jointed legs and hard exoskeletons

blood platelets—microscopic disks in the blood that aid in coagulation

capillaries—tiny tubes that carry blood

carbon dioxide—a gas produced during respiration

cartilage—a firm yet elastic material often located at the ends of bones

circulatory system—the system that moves blood through an animal's body

cocoon—a protective case made of silk or similar materials

denticles—small, pointed ridges on the exoskeleton of an arthropod

dissolved—turned into a solution

ectoparasites—parasites that live on the outside of other animals

egg—the first stage in the life cycle of many animals

endoparasites—parasites that live inside other animals

enzyme—a complex protein that aids in specific biochemical reactions, such as digestion

exoskeleton—a hard covering on the outside of an animal

feces—solid body waste

fluke—a parasitic flatworm

follicle—a cavity in which a single hair grows

glucose—a type of sugar that is common in nature

hermaphroditic—having both male and female sex organs

hirudin—an anticoagulant in the saliva of leeches

host—an animal that provides a place to live for a parasite

hypostome—the front parts of a tick's head

incisors—teeth that are used primarily for cutting

lactic acid—a waste product produced by animals when they sweat

larva—the second stage in the development of some animals

metamorphosis—the stages of development through which an animal passes as it becomes an adult

nits—the eggs of a louse

nocturnal—active at night

nymph—the larva of an insect that undergoes incomplete metamorphosis

palpi—tiny sensory feelers on the heads of certain insects

parasites—organisms that obtain most or all of their nourishment from other organisms and are harmful to their hosts

plague—an epidemic disease with a high death rate

plasma—a pale, yellowish fluid in which red and white blood cells are suspended

proboscis—a nose or noselike appendage

proteins—complex substances that are necessary for proper growth in plants and animals

pupa—the third stage in the development of some animals, especially insects

questing behavior—the behavior of a dormant tick that is waiting for food

red blood cells—blood cells that carry oxygen to various body parts

saliva—a liquid produced in the salivary glands and secreted in the mouth to aid in the digestive process

species—a group of living things that have many common characteristics

trachea—a tube that carries inhaled air to the lungs of an animal

vector—an organism that spreads disease

vertebrate—an animal with a backbone

white blood cells—blood cells that fight off infections

To Find
Out More

Books

Else, George. *Insects and Spiders*. New York: Time-Life Books, 1997.

Facklam, Howard, and Margery Facklam. *Parasites*. New York: Twenty-First Century Books, 1994.

Fredericks, Anthony D. *Cannibal Animals: Animals That Eat Their Own Kind*. Danbury, CT: Franklin Watts, 1999.

———— and Sneed Collard, Eds. *Amazing Animals*. Minnetonka, MN: NorthWord Press, 2000.

Knapp, Ron. *Bloodsuckers*. Springfield, NJ: Enslow Publishers, 1996.

Merrick, Patrick. *Leeches*. Chanhassen, MN: The Child's World, 2001.

Seidensticker, John, and Susan Lumpkin. *Dangerous Animals*. New York: Time-Life Books, 1995.

Video

Creepy Creatures, National Geographic Society.

The Predators (4-video collection), National Geographic Society.

Nightmares of Nature (4-video collection), National Geographic Society.

CD-ROMs

Looking at Living Things, National Geographic Society. IBM & Macintosh.

Microsoft Dangerous Creatures, Microsoft Corporation. IBM and Macintosh.

Organizations and Online Sites

American Zoo and Aquarium Association
8403 Colesville Road, Suite 710
Silver Spring, MD 20910
http://www.aza.org
This group is dedicated to the advancement of zoos and aquariums in the areas of conservation, education, science, and recreation.

Defenders of Wildlife
1101 14th Street NW, Suite 1400
Washington, D.C. 20005
http://www.defenders.org/
This organization is dedicated to the protection of all wild animals and plants in their natural environment.

National Audubon Society
700 Broadway
New York, NY 10013
http://www.audubon.org/
This group focuses on research and education that helps protect and save threatened ecosystems.

National Wildlife Federation
1400 Sixteenth Street NW
Washington, D.C. 20036

http://www.nwf.org/

This organization works to promote environmental awareness and to help conserve natural resources.

The Nature Conservatory
4245 North Fairfax Drive, Suite 100
Arlington, VA 22203-1606
http://nature.org

This international organization is committed to preserving biological diversity by protecting natural lands and the life they harbor.

The Wildlife Conservation Society
2300 Southern Blvd.
Bronx, NY 10460
http://wcs.org/

This group is dedicated to preserving biodiversity, teaching ecology, and inspiring care for all wildlife.

The Wildlife Society
5410 Grosvenor Lane
Bethesda, MD 20814
http://www.wildlife.org

This is an international non-profit scientific and educational association dedicated to excellence in wildlife stewardship through science and education.

A Note on Sources

I frequently get ideas for my children's books by talking to students. As a children's author, I travel around the country making presentations at school assemblies and giving writing workshops. In each school I visit, I ask students to suggest ideas for future books. I have discovered that some of my best ideas come from the people who will be reading the books.

The idea for this book came from a group of students I visited in Florida. I shared with them all the research I did for a book entitled *Cannibal Animals*. I told them how I read lots of nature magazines, such as *International Wildlife*, *Nature Conservancy*, *Wildlife Conservation*, and *Discover*. I mentioned some of the research I did on the Internet, as well as all the scientists and librarians I contacted around the country looking for sources and information. I also told them about all the children's books, science books, and magazine articles I read during my research. They learned why all this work was important to the writing of a book as well as to its accuracy.

In several discussions, I asked the students if they had questions about the world of nature in general or about certain kinds of animals. Among other things, they told me that they had never seen any books about bloodsucking creatures and wanted to know if I knew any. I told them I did not but said that I would look for some. When I returned home, I discovered that there were few books about this fascinating topic. So I began to do some research. I called scientists, looked in dozens of books at my local public library, spent a lot of time surfing the Web, and gathered information from conferences, magazine articles, and professors with whom I teach.

As you might imagine, I discovered some very interesting material. The more I discovered, the more I knew that I wanted to share this data with readers just like you. So, I began to write this book. It took lots of time and lots of effort, but it was worth it. After almost a year of research and more than a year of writing, the book was completed. For me, this has been an exciting voyage of discovery and exploration. I hope you enjoy it as much as I did.

I would like to extend my sincere appreciation to Ronald A. Nussbaum, who reviewed the text for scientific accuracy. His comments and suggestions were invaluable during the revision process.

—Anthony D. Fredericks

Index

Numbers in *italics* indicate illustrations.

About the Author

Anthony D. Fredericks is a nationally known children's author. His assemblies and school visits have captivated thousands of elementary students and their teachers from coast to coast. Fredericks's background includes extensive experience as a classroom teacher, author, professional storyteller, and university specialist in elementary science methods. He has written more than twenty children's books. His Franklin Watts credits include the best-selling *Cannibal Animals: Animals That Eat Their Own Kind* and *Bloodsucking Creatures*. Fredericks is currently a professor of education at York College in York, Pennsylvania.